Stade

Sales Guide to Riches

Deluxe Edition

"The most simplified guide to building lasting relationships with your market.

Maintain complete control over your sales process and achieve a win-win for you & your clients."

-Derek Staden

-The <u>NEW</u> **"2 Slow is Painful"** Deluxe Edition-

Staden's

Sales Guide to Riches

Deluxe Edition

ISBN # 978-1-365-67724-3

Published by Lulu.com

Preface…………………………….......pg.4

My story……………………….……pg.10

Why sales as a profession?…………….pg.32

Do you have a Hustle or Business?….....pg.35

Do I need a Business Plan?……………pg.36

Product Development………….…..…….pg.37

Demographics/Target Market……..…..pg.38

Market Share………………………….pg.40

Sizzling Presentation….…..…………...pg.48

Handling Objections……....………...pg.56

Useful Scripts……….………..…….pg.60-69

Who is a Salesperson?……..…………pg.71

Important Terms……………….…...pg.82

Closes……………………….………pg 83-88

F.O.R.M./S.T.E.A.M………………..…...89-90

2 Slow is Painful………...……………pg. 93

Preface

We are natural **actors**, that are capable of subconsciously (and *with minimal effort*), adjusting to the varied circumstances that present themselves each day of our lives.

We are at times thought of as loving parents, the nagging child, a wise Elder, or maybe even a demanding Boss.
We were just born to *function* this way.

Maybe, we are genetically pre-disposed to be great actors. I believe that for many, this ability to adapt to societal stressors, is a skill that can be harnessed to become a very successful sales consultant!

So, why is it so difficult for **most** people to memorize or even master a *basic Sales Process*?

There are **many** *legitimate* obstacles that I have personally had to navigate, on my journey to sales mastery.

Having personally overcome these challenges, we can properly educate you on how to:

1) Internalize your sales process (script)
2) Share ideas on how to make it fit "you"
3) Then help you to replicate OUR results

New sales people often have a pre-existing, fear-of-rejection when it comes to sales! Most are uncomfortable with approaching a prospective client, or calling on friends to inform them on their new product or service. This type of *fear* can infect the mind of the sales person thereby, preventing them from effectively building a client base. This must be addressed upfront. And we must.

Without building your confidence, you will find it very difficult to execute in your sales process **or** get "a commitment" for the sale.

There may be **many** uncomfortable and embarrassing moments. It's okay. We have all faced this reality.

To avoid these undesirable moments some of you may prefer to be fully competent with a new sales process before, you speak to anyone. We understand why many feel this way. We have learned that speaking to people right away will give you immediate feedback on what you are instinctively strong at and what you need to improve.

Lastly, there may exist a select group of you, that desire a little encouragement from a qualified coach, a guide that can be referenced and you are ready to hit the ground running. You may from time to time seek guidance as needed, to help steer you along the way.

Well no matter where you are in your belief about your ability to learn our process, we can meet you where you are. I believe that I am that coach for some, we have this guide that can be a tool to direct others but, all of you will obtain information on strategies to help you navigate the mental and emotional maze on your journey to master <u>your</u> *new* sales process.

So, we ask you:

- What do you <u>expect</u> from your sales career?
- What is your <u>action plan</u> to reach your goals?
- What's <u>prevented</u> you in the past?

I believe in you. Most of your friends & family believe in you. The question is…do you believe in you?

If you study this system and, it makes sense to you, adds value to your business or goals and lastly…you can see how it may allow you to earn great money, tell me, would you follow it?

I've had several great mentors. I've been fortunate to experience recognition & great financial success.

I have been allowed to travel (most of the time with my family), to sales seminars & exotic getaways for reaching monthly, quarterly and yearly sales goals.

I am most grateful for having enjoyed these experiences. Although, I remember how difficult it was for me to pick up a phone to set appointments, when I started my career!

I once faced extreme *anguish* and "paralyzing" *fear* from just the mere *thought* of calling on a prospect. ***I had to figure out how to fix it?***

Very early in life I was told, **"if you don't work, you don't eat"**. Not directly but through my observations.

So many people suffer and <u>our</u> families may suffer because the leaders of our family aren't willing to work smart enough or practice consistently enough, to overcome their fears. We ALL face daily internal struggles. In our personal sales journey, we must find a way to improve our skills, fight hard(er) for our personal and family goals so, we can win!

Starting today there is NO more **fear** or **doubt**...because now we will tell ourselves positive messages and believe in our abilities. We love people. They need our help. We want to help them. So we will prepare for success, fight fearlessly and win!

When I was young I was told to **"get a job, any job and work hard at it"**!

After hearing this statement, I focused on staying employed, but I eventually discovered that hard work is not always rewarded from maintaining "constant" employment. So, I have made a vow that I would not be a victim of laziness, or bad circumstance or find myself constantly blaming "the man" for my situation!

I had no problem with the "JOB" **thang** until, one day I got injured at work, <u>and</u> didn't have any benefits. After this event things would change dramatically but it would eventually reach a positive outcome.

Let me tell you a story, (a short but true story) about how I grew my income from $3.35 per hour, to earning $23k in my last <u>month</u> in the sales industry. (And over $50k in my last 3 months!) It was a wild ride.

I want to tell you the <u>good</u> & the <u>bad</u>. You may be encouraged that since we survived it, and had some success, that you can too.

So, here's my story:

I was born in Jackson, Ga a small rural community in Butts County, just 35 minutes south of Atlanta, Ga.

As a young kid (4 yrs. old) I noticed that my mother, held a job or two and also attended school part-time. (She was focused on taking care of us, no matter what she had to do) She would catch the bus, walk and study day and night. I am thankful to her for her sacrifices.

We would spend our days watching cars go by. We would spend time playing with our pets and having fun with our childhood friends and relatives.

When we became teenagers, we finally had the opportunity to work with my Grandfather, Leroy Head Sr! We always wanted to work for him. Everyone in the city wanted to work for my Grandfather.

What a great privilege this was for us!

My Grandfather was fun to be around and he never punished us. We never wanted to go home at the end of our work day.

My Grandfather gave us delicious lunches complete with candy, pop or whatever we wanted for dessert. It was a dream job! Every day was a fantastic experience. We also earned some fantastic summer cash!

Sounds like fun doesn't? It **was** fun even thou we worked very hard every day! We usually did the job of an adult, for usually 10 to 12 hours a day. We looked forward to grinding it out every day!

As teenager's we made approximately $5/hr (In 1983 the minimum wage was $3.35)

We had no idea that we were getting paid

better than some adults, until my Mom brought it to our attention. Thinking about the money that we were making, I always wondered what type of money my Granddad was making in this business?

I didn't know how he got started in this business **or** who taught him about this business. I did understand what his business <u>was</u>: In his business he would buy 55/gallon steel oil drums & wooden pallets, fix them, clean them and resale them.

Sounds simple enough doesn't it.

Not only was I unable to figure out how he put it together, I noticed that he never seemed to work that hard, which puzzled me more. Later I would be shocked to discover how much income he actually earned.

He earned 5 figures per week consistently!

He was very good at delegating work that needed to be done. He rewarded us for going above and beyond the call of duty.

He was a master at building <u>personal relationships</u>! Maybe this was the reason that he **<u>seemed</u>** to do very little work.

Maybe the work that I observed was the toughest work that a business owner must do…which is to manage personalities.

My Granddad was well respected. Most of my grandfather's employees would kill themselves to impress him. Producing great results was usually followed by a reward, a cash bonus or "Atta Boys" from my Granddad. (which was just as satisfying)

I zoom forward a few years (and now) I am in my late teens. After working several retail jobs, I began to reflect back upon my choices for my respective jobs & careers.

My first choice was a famous burger restaurant which offered me a discounted lunch and a $3.35/hour wage.

I worked hard and was always tired but I could never recall having any significant savings. After working several other retail and restaurant jobs, I had ***enough***, I was fed up and decided to go <u>back</u> to work with my

Grandfather. This time I decided to work with him full-time.

After finishing High School, I felt that this would be an excellent chance to excel while working with my Grandfather.

My thinking was, that if I worked hard, I could make a tremendous wage and save some money, for the car I really wanted and maybe get my own place?

I quickly found out that my Grandfather paid me a little different as an adult. He paid me based on my production??? I was excited and nervous because I'd never been paid that way. Hourly wage I understood. But, production was based on results. This was no big deal because I worked hard…but now I had to work fast as well.

What if I couldn't cut it? What if this new

job he gave me was too difficult for me?

I figured if my older cousins and his other adult employees could "hack" it, surely, I could. I was a wrestler, baseball and football player in High School. I was fit and I believed myself to be fierce! So, I pushed myself to work hard.

My belief system was that I could do anything that anyone else could do and I would do it exceptionally well.

I focused and due to my competitive mindset, I was making more money than I had ever made...doing any other job!

He paid me well and I made a few extra dollars almost every day. Everything was going really well until, one hot summer day, I was tired and rushing and lost focus.

After a disagreement with my Stepfather, I moved in with my Grandparents. The good thing was now whenever there was extra work I had a great chance at getting it.

I think I was a little distracted with my living situation and working hard to save to get my own place. It was a very hot day. I was working on repairing pallets with a power nail gun, and the nail skipped off the edge of the pallet, through the table and down through the top of my right foot!

Without going into the bloody details, I was told that my Grandfather had **no** health insurance on me as an employee. I also, didn't have any significant savings built up yet to pay any medical bills.

I no other choice but to call my mother and ask for help. I was 18yrs old and "acted like a man" (at least I thought so). I wanted to stand on my own. I made good money but, I couldn't handle tough situations. By the way what was this **Health Insurance** thing**?**

Why didn't they just let me go to the hospital and pay over an extended period of time? My Mom was upset (and rightfully so) she met me at the hospital, got my bill squared away, then she gave my Grandfather the blues. This is when I remembered: If you are hurt, you can't work which also equals...

"If you Don't work, you Don't eat".

So, what did I learn:

-Sometimes a JOB will not meet your needs.

-You can work your behind off and you will rarely out earn the person that owns the company you work for.

-The business owner has no vested interest in teaching the ins and outs of their business.

-It's wise to have emergency savings!

After my injury, I relaxed until it was time to enter into the Air Force in 1989.

I served in Desert Storm. And after my service was complete I spent some time in the music business. That was amazing!

Unfortunately, I was in a recording session working on a project for submission to a record label then, I received a call that my step father was very ill and that I should come home. I got home from New York to Atlanta right away, to find that he had passed.

After the funeral my mother informed me that he didn't have any **Life Insurance**! He owned Funeral Homes, in two different cities. And he had been in business for over 20 years. How could this happen? My Mom faced challenging times financially.

She fought hard. I felt helpless. My brother and I couldn't do anything significant to make it better for her.

I eventually moved back to the mid-west and got a job working in a warehouse in Kansas. One day while working diligently, I received a page (This is before cellphones).

I called the number back and it was an old Air Force buddy who told me to call him

ASAP! Oh man, what could possibly be going on??? I was really concerned.

When I called, he asked me for my address. I was puzzled. Typically, I expect to receive money when someone asks for my address.

So, I gave it to him. He said he was going to send me some information and that I should look at it right away. He asked me to call him at home.

So, I got his information and called him. He sent me copies of checks that he earned from something called **commissions**???

What are "commissions" that was a new word for me. I'd heard of commissions before, but I never worked a commission-based job. So, when I spoke to my friend, I acted as If I understood how commissions worked, (I didn't) and I could not believe the size of these checks. Some of these checks were over $1,000...to sell CARS??? That was amazing to me!

I tried to reserve myself. I told him if he could do it then I could do it, so what do I have to do? I was ready to get more information and get started.

So, I drove from Kansas to Louisiana with hopes of making it big in sales. He helped me find a place to stay and took me to the dealership the night before I was scheduled to interview for the position.

When we got to the dealership, I thought it was odd that we could be there after hours. He explained how to sell each car in the showroom and how the commissions worked. It was a little confusing but the money sounded so good, I told him that he had my attention, and I would make it work.

After a week of struggling along, I finally got in stride. When I got my first check, I was happy and confused at the same time.

I worked 80 hours and only made $750! It was ok money but I finally understood that commissions were definitely a "If you don't work you don't eat" situation.

I got better and soon I was having some $1,000 weekly checks just like my friend. Finally, it hit me, if "you do more, you get more"! This was fantastic! This is when I finally became a "sales representative".

After earning an average of $4k/month, I wanted more. I learned to sell everything, Computers, Clothing, Vitamins, Soaps etc.

I tried all types of commission plans and structures. Finally, I came back to an established Rent-a-Car leasing company just outside of Atlanta, Ga.

The company was very reputable. I was offered and accepted a **salary** for the first time in my life. This was not what I thought it was. I worked 55 to 60 hours per week and my paycheck stayed the same. This was not a good discovery for me.

We had sales quotas for up-sales and insurance sales. We could win lunch, certificates and plaques for selling insurance products but we didn't receive any extra compensation or commissions. I usually led the store in sales but, it didn't reflect in my paycheck. How can you work such long hours and not make more money even if you do your job exceptionally?

One day while cleaning a car to prepare it for delivery to a customer, I sprayed tire cleaner in my eyes. Horrible experience. I said to myself, here we go again.

I went to the hospital and this time the INSURANCE from work did pick it up...yeah! This insurance thing is not so bad.

While I was out recovering, I got a call from my old Air Force buddy.

Yes, the same buddy that got me involved in sales originally. He faxed me some new check stubs from a new company and WOW...although the checks were smaller he had received several of them that month!

He had a month where he earned 20 plus commission checks, that added up to nearly $5k! This was even more amazing to me!

Bills came all throughout the month so it was great to see the ability to make checks almost every day of the month!

All I needed to know is **if** they had an office in Atlanta. They did. I started with this new company and in 2 weeks from the time I completed my initial training, I earned $4,200! This ruined me forever!

I quit my full-time job with the Rental Car Company and made a commitment to study hard to grow my skills.

That's when I became a **<u>Sales Consultant</u>**.

After a couple of years of successful sales years, traveling the country and helping hundreds of families with my financial services products, a tragic event happened...Sept 11th 2001. We really struggled. Everyone did. This was discouraging and I very confused about people's reaction to the tragedy. People were afraid and uneasy. After several tough months things got a little better. In 2003, we had to deal with the loss of my brother, who was active duty and was preparing to fight the "war on terror".

This was a very dark time for my mother and myself. It is not something that I would ever want to experience again.

I was upset for quite a while and lost focus with my business. I experienced some tough financial times, and learned a lot about my will to fight. We eventually recovered again.

We would receive one more gut punch...this was the most challenging of all (in business), the market crash and mortgage crisis of 2008!

This was an unbelievably tough time in the sales industry for myself and most of my colleagues. In my mind I wanted to quit, but my family was so supportive and needed my extra effort. I had no choice but to keep moving. My family believed in me. And I decided to fight harder for them, I really had no choice.

I was tired of struggling. I knew that being in sales was the best way to feed my family and provide for a future but I needed to have a more secure and stable service to offer. This is time that I evolved into a **<u>Sales Professional</u>**!

One of the best days of my career happened one cool fall day, I received a call from one of my former mentors. He mentioned how well he was doing working with seniors in Medicare that needed senior health plans.

I allowed him to teach me the ropes. I researched, trained for hard, then I got my own agency. I begin to teach and consult Medicare-aged Seniors, with their children involved every step of the way. I wanted to help them make better choices for their retirement. I gave them free Medicare policy, Life Insurance and Retirement account reviews, to earn their trust. I built strong relationships.

I provided a financial needs analysis portfolio to each family member.

All of a sudden, in a matter of 4 years, I went from struggling to make $1k to earning $2,500 a month. Then I was able to earn $5,000 and eventually $7,500!

In no time at all I was earning $10,000 plus and in my final month before retirement I earned $23k! I retired officially when I started to receive treatment for my Military injuries and allowed my license to expire in 2010 ending a great run in the Insurance industry. During this process, I became a **Sales Professional**. I learned to build strong personal and business relationships.

I was truly a professional at my craft. After many years away from my career in sales, I really missed my clients. I felt compelled to write this book to help other struggling sales professionals to master the fundamentals in sales. It was and always has been about my clients and my teammates. Now I teach unofficially. I still help Seniors and others with research and support.

I mastered the steps to becoming a Sales Professional. If you commit there is nothing that can stop you. There will be sacrifices or exchanges that you will need to make and investments of time and resources but bet on you. Other professionals have accomplished great things, in their sales career, so why not you? I am going to share some important concepts with you. Take notes in the book.

Highlight it and write all over it. This is your guide.

I have a few questions?

Do you **want** to become a Sales professional? Will you face adversity and not allow it to stop you? Will you want to quit every day, for weeks at a time? The answer to these 3 questions hopefully is YES! But if you are up for one of the most challenging & rewarding experiences of your life, so if you have courage, let's begin.

There is a difference between an Associate, a Consultant and a Professional. Mainly, the consultant gives advice and relies on his/her credentials to elicit trust from the customer.

A Professional, on the other hand, usually provides value by extracting information from the customer and selling to those exposed needs. They observe the potential client's behavior during the presentation and deliver a "sizzling" presentation which educates the prospect and builds credibility. They also, fight hard to earn referrals.

What do you want? What can stop you from achieving your goals? Do you believe you can have your goals? Do you need help setting goals? If you have these questions, we would like to help you.

I want to help you avoid the pain that I experienced. As you have read it was <u>not</u> easy for me (It <u>was</u> simple). There is a difference and in time you will learn the difference between simple and easy.

I had a system to follow. It had been proven to work by others. All I needed to do was commit to follow it, then get busy.

Let's commit today that you will follow this plan to the letter. You will **<u>commit</u>** to having success. When you move, you should move on purpose. Remember to also have fun! If you aren't having fun then you are WORKING and working in not fun.

I dedicate this book to my Brother & Mom:

Sgt. Christopher Staden (Brother/deceased)
And my mother
Ms. Irma Head Blake (Mom)

Notes:

Why sales as a profession?

"If I had to list all the reasons why you should become a sales professional as well as the reasons that you shouldn't, There would be a longer list for <u>not</u> becoming a sales professional"

-Derek Staden

Let's see:

Hourly wage? (Paid based on time spent)

Salary? (Based on workload management)

Commissions? (Paid based on RESULTS!)

Show up, stay out of trouble and you are guaranteed to make a wage. Follow the system at your job and continue to make money. This sounds comfortable.

So why Commissions? There are no guarantees. It requires special training and skills. Who would want to put themselves in such a situation when trying to provide for their family?

If a company sells a product or service and YOU have an opportunity to offer that product to the public and receive a piece of the revenue…that is a FANTASTIC opportunity!

You are one of the most important employees/partners to the owner's business.

There may be bonuses, incentives & other rewards if you make a commitment to win!

You make $8/hr. to sell business suits. After 8 hour's you have earned $64! If you sell 10 suits or 1 suit, you make $64. The manager or owner may provide a bonus as an incentive to get more production out of you but let's explore commissions.

or

You make 20% commission. You sell 10 suits @ $100 per suit that equals = $200! The same salesperson sells 1 suit they only make $20! This is a dynamic opportunity.

*In one scenario, they make $44 less with the opportunity to make $136 more!

If this makes you excited, continue to get more information. Maybe sales **is** for you. Maybe you could consider owning a sales business. You must become strong in sales first, then you hire, train and develop other committed sales partners! If executed successfully this is a very lucrative way to earn a living. Again, simple but not easy.

We will discuss ways to make this process simple by utilizing this guide.

If you have a product that you believe in, go apply for a job to sell that product. If you have an interest in Sales and you would like to see how well you do in it, give it a shot.

Do you have a <u>Hustle</u> or a <u>Business?</u>

<u>What is a Hustle?</u> In my definition, it is a way to make money without the structure and rigors of managing a complete "sales or business system".

You find a product or service, prep it, package it, and sell it. It is a sheer numbers game. In time, you may develop approaches that work better than others.

<u>What is a Business?</u> It is a system that is setup to function effectively regardless of the individual skills and abilities of the employees that make up the business.

It does require highly skilled management and talented owners, but the majority of the workforce can be novice and have minimal experience.

As a note, most people that operate hustles don't commit to pay taxes, get licensed or certified. Their focus is to move products and make money.

A business has a vision, stated goals and a system to manage people and results!

Let's continue to get more information.

Do I need a Business Plan?

If you plan on legitimately operating a business you need a business plan. One of the main reasons to own a business plan is to gather all of your systems, goals and actions into one presentation.

You want to properly present to lenders, supporters and investors your vision & mission. Another purpose of a business plan is to layout your company's revenue streams and your company's production capability. If you plan on operating a Hustle you can avoid the investment of creating a biz plan.

Product Development

When considering a Business Plan, you should work on several important steps in your preparation. Some people believe you should work on your Demographics first but I believe and advise that you perfect your product or service offering. This ensures that you have a viable product before making the huge investment of developing a business plan or commissioning a Demographics study. There are steps to Developing a supreme product. We will discuss this further in our Business Development Class.

In short:

We all have an area of focus that we can see ourselves working in. As salespeople or small business owners we must look at our area of focus and find out what brings us the most joy in that area of focus.

Ex: (Area of focus) <u>Teaching</u> specifically Sales Training is my "bullseye" or focus. We should think of a product of service that solves a problem for others and fits within <u>our</u> area of focus.

Research on a career website the career field that you desire to be in and find your focus!

<u>Demographics</u>

As you work to fully-develop your product or service, you need to also discover what the people that live in your area, potentially need or want from your product.

How many men, women or children (under 18) live in your area? What are the largest age groups ex: 18-25, 26-55 or 56 and older? What are the racial groups and their percentage of the population of your city.

There are several other groups or classes that you could use to analyze the makeup of your community or city.

Your purpose for doing this is to identify how your market is constructed so, you can strategically select a Target Market. Once you identify a Target Market you can more efficiently promote your product or service to that market.

Think of a Dartboard. You have five red target areas on the board with the highest amount of points awarded to hitting the center bullseye!

Your Target Market **is** that bullseye, and the Dartboard is your Demographics.

Market Share

This section will deal with the opportunities that exist in your target market. This section is very important toward establishing your revenue goals and profit projections.

For example:

You discover that your Demographics state that there are 10,000 black female adults over 25 in your market.

Further research shows that of this group 5,000 (or half) do some form of exercise.

You create a new exercise bike that caters to females which allows them to stay in touch with their social media, develop menus, watch television programming and scroll through their day planner /calendar all from the comfort of a seated position on a state of the art computerized stationary bike.

You determine that you want to reach a minimum of 2,000 of those 5,000 ladies. So you set a goal to market to all 5,000 ladies and establish your revenue goals to reflect acquiring at minimum the 2,000 customers.

This is an abbreviated summary of establishing your Market Share.

Outline to the Sales Process

A. Income Goals (Daily/ Weekly/ Monthly)

It's been stated to you many times in your life..."Before you reach your destination, you must first know WHERE you are going".

So, we must have a clear mental picture of what we expect from this new sales process. Hopefully, seeing yourself making a lot of money is high on that list. If it's not high on your list, then call, email, or track me down to get...YOUR MONEY BACK!

We are in the Sales Industry to help people and to make money,,,a lot of Money! Why else would we punish ourselves by being involved in such a mentally challenging career??? Don't be ashamed of making money. Everybody does it. Why not you?

Alright let's talk about...What amount of income do we NEED daily & weekly for our families? When developing our list, we should consider only our <u>NEEDS</u>. (unlike our *WANTS*, our needs are non-negotiable)

If we fill up a list with WANTS, what will usually happen is we will not **<u>fight</u>** as hard to achieve them. "WANTS are DREAMS but NEEDS are GOALS".

Example: How much Food do I need, monthly Utilities, Gas for my Car, Loans on House or Car, Clothing for Work, Health/Life Insurance do you need...you get the picture?

When you set your Goals, ensure that you add 10% - 20% to your goals for emergency fund savings. (Remember the nail in the foot episode) *If you skip anything in this guide you may become lost. So don't. (Lol)

Some of us may not be familiar with setting financial goals. Some of us may tend to be a little too aggressive. Some of us, don't seem to have an idea of WHAT to put on our goal sheet! So be realistic!

If you've never made a six-figure income, lets first shoot for replacing your current income, then gradually move your goals up.

We should "Walk before we run."

(Don't say, "Crawl before you walk" because frankly that's as painful as a JOB!)

Sometimes we don't ***know it all*** but we should still move forward and trust the steps to our "Sales System".

This monthly number that we are looking for is called your "NEED NUMBER".

So, let's say your NEED NUMBER comes up to $3000 monthly.

First you would add 20%, (Emergency Fund contribution) which is $600.

That's a total of $3600 monthly! This is your families NEED number!

So, what if you only make $1,500 on your full-time job? No problem. $1,500 plus $600 (for emergency fund savings) from your sales job/business, combined with the $1,500 that you already earn from your full-time job equals YOUR MONTHLY GOAL or NEED number of $3,600!

$1,500 Job + $2,100 Sales Biz =$3,600

So, initially you will subsidize your full-time job by mastering this sales process then, REPLACE your full-time job by making the entire $3,600 with your sales business. *As you read earlier, this is how I became full-time and self-employed.

B. Set Daily, Weekly, Monthly "Time Commitment" Goals

If you want to be effective, it is vital that

you manage your time wisely. We will keep this section simple and clear. If you know what income you want to earn, and know what time you can commit to work your sales business, then the battle is half over!

If you have discovered that it takes 10 phone calls to get 3 contacts to pick up the phone, then you only need to figure out how much time it takes to make those 10 calls and engage those 3 prospects.

Ex: If you make 10 straight phone calls before you take a break and discover that you get 3 people to engage you in a conversation about your product or service that would be:

1) 10 Calls takes about (10 minutes)

2) 3 Calls engaged in conversation (15 mins)

3) 1 Appt. set/1 "committed to buy" (5 min.)

That's only 30 minutes per day! Sure, you can get one client per day.

The magic happens when you realize that you should and can work your sales business like "a job". Treat it with respect. Work!

Who says you can't make appointments for 2 or 3 hours and still have an exceptional week of income???

Now all you need to do is run these numbers out based on your daily hours worked then weekly and finally on a monthly basis.

Because of the work involved, most sales reps never make it past this point. If they could only understand how close they were to making the incredible life of their dreams.

If they understood that the prospect or potential client, "CAN ONLY TELL YOU YES or NO"! They will not hurt you.

They will not spit on you, kick you out of their house. (Unless you are rude) So... breathe, slow down, and ask questions when you don't know what to do or say. Study this manual and it will come to you. Read this manual (3) TIMES completely, then call us for clarity!

Also, study this manual at least 30 to 45 minutes a day regardless of your current results!!!!!!!!!

C. Track your activity

Each day, at the end of the day, you should review your results. Look at how many calls you made, how many prospects engaged you on the phone, then how many you got committed to move along into the Sales Process toward a sale!

This can be done with either a Time Management Software Program or Day planner booklet.

Track your time spent on the phones setting appointments. Time spent actually selling, getting referrals, completing "Thank You" cards, when you were making follow-up phone calls etc...

This will show you how much you are truly earning based upon the actual hours worked. (Which doesn't include breaks or lunch)

D. Sizzling Presentation

You sit down across from the potential client. You are nervous and short of breath. Will I remember their names? Will I remember how to share my products? Will I make a sale? (There are many opportunities to fail or make mistakes). Just Relax.

So many things are racing through your head. Its ok, stay calm and remember that you are just beginning. Even if you've been in sales for 20 years, THIS is new to you. So, tell everyone that you are new (all of your clients) and that you are still learning. Then tell yourself. Now there is no pressure.

Go ahead and do it...make mistakes and fail moving forward!

Giving a presentation can be daunting. So many things to remember. Fear not, we have a simple way to remember what you should do.

Follow these steps below:

1.   Compliment "Prospect" -Ask questions about their home, car, kids, neighborhood etc... Show a genuine interest. Make note.

2.   *F.O.R.M.- Ask about the prospective clients'... (Family, Occupation, Recreation, Motivations) -Ask questions about these four topics and you understand them better and you will win them over. This information will come in handy later when you prepare to close them. (Ask at least 2 questions apiece about each topic) You don't have to go in any particular order.

(Examples given later in the book)

3.   Seat Positioning -Offer the prospects the option of sitting on their comfortable couch and visiting for a few hours or

moving to the kitchen table where you can lay things out level where they can be easily seen and get out of the way in 30 to 45 minutes. Always sit were you are facing the family on one side of the table and never sit between the prospects. You will not be able to properly observe both prospects (When the couple wants to communicate secret messages visually to one another, it is easier when you are not directly in front of them).

4.   Share your Personal Story (Tell your Why?)-Explain briefly why YOU are in this industry and with this company.

5.   Prepare the prospect for Referrals-"I will complete a presentation in a second and I would like to hand you a piece of paper, if you could, as I share about what we do please list at least 10 to 15 referrals of people that you know that may benefit from my product/service. I don't need the phone numbers right now. Just the names.

If you appreciate the "no pressure" approach that we provide to you and you appreciate your results I will ask for permission to reach out to them.

They will not be obligated to buy a product or service from me. My business survives on referrals so if you don't mind, I would love to see if you and I could help them?"

6.   Company Overview -Share brief history of your Company and highlight the positives of your history and your past successes. Share the Company Concepts, specialty products and services. You should also cover the Company Compensation.

7.   If I could, would you? -If I can provide a solution to solve all of the issues that you mentioned with your current product that makes sense to you, and creates additional value that you are not currently receiving and you feel that it makes sense to you, saves you money, what would prevent you from allowing me to help you?

8.   Handle objections by asking Who, What, When, Where, How & Why? You can use what's called, the "Hot Potato" which is a handling objections technique. Discuss later.

9.   Ask for their business-I can get you started today with a check if that's ok, or will a credit card, work better for you?

10.   W.F.A.-Wait for Answer (Be prepared to address any Objections that arise)

*(You will learn how to ask *S.T.E.A.M. questions later in the book, to get referrals.)*

11.   Complete the Application-Get method of payment.

12.   Get more referrals. "Do you have a cellphone?" (Wait for Answer) Great! Roughly how many names do you have in your contact list on your phone? Wait for answer. No matter what the say respond with: "Great! I don't need that many, normally I am only able to get to 20 or 30

people all month. "How many do you think you can come up with, 60 referrals are the most that I've received in one visit?"

13.   Thank the Family-"Thank you for the trust you have given us to help your family, here is my card. I will be available during business hours to answer any questions and resolve any issues that you may have. If I am able to help your friends and family, I will treat them with the same respect that I/we displayed today. Thank you for the referrals that you provided, is there anyone else that you can think of that may see value in our product?"

E. Tracking Results/Production

When you go through the lengthy process of obtaining a new client, you want to make sure that you keep a log of your results. How many appointments, referrals, phone calls and contacts are very important but none more important than your production or sales!

Make sure you are paying close attention to the hours you are investing and compare it to the revenue generated. If the numbers are not satisfactory, increase the calls by 1 hour/day until you meet your goals weekly.

Purchase a log book at your local office supply store and chart your production.

F. Send Thank You Cards

Most people will ignore this step and that's why most people will not make $20k in a month! You must find ways to separate yourself from other sales professionals. Your client is always one nice phone call, bad experience or thank you card away from talking to another company.

It doesn't matter what kind or color, just send them. Birthday's, anniversary, kid's birthdays, be unique! All sales representatives send _cards_ on holidays, so you be different do something unique.

Handling Objections

I would like to give some useful information on how to handle your prospects objections to making a purchase with you!

First, when a client doesn't want to move forward with the sales process, an objection or obstacle has been created to reaching a sell. It could be verbal: "I don't have any money" or it can be non-verbal: Like shaking their head from side to side with their arms crossed with an intense stare.

When your prospective client presents an objection, it is up to you to address and move forward to the sell.

1.   When you receive an objection, isolate it, acknowledge it, then ask a probing question (open-ended questions that evoke a long response) like: Why do you feel you can't afford our service, at this time? or What is making you uncomfortable with this process? When do you think, you will be ready? Now that you have done this the

prospect can vent and breathe. (This can be difficult.) Let them. Let them talk until they don't have anything left to say. Do not interrupt them. Listen carefully.

2.   Now you ask a few more clarifying questions. (i.e.: questions that help you better understand what the real problem is. *Yes or No questions like: I understand that you are not ready to move forward today; was it me? was the presentation confusing? or is there something that you would like for me to clarify?

3.   Whenever the client asks you a question, respond by repeating their question so that they know you are listening to them. Then immediately ask a clarifying question. This technique keeps you in control and allows you time to think clearly and find your answer. This technique is called "Hot potato". (They, throw a question toward you and you "catch it" and throw one back) Once you have done this and found

the real objection, you can phrase your solution in the form of a question like this:

"Now that we have uncovered that there was a misunderstanding with how you thought our product worked, I would like to ask if I could clarify how it properly functions to your satisfaction. Is there any reason why you wouldn't allow me to earn your business today?" WFA (Wait for Answer)

There are so many strategies and choices to addressing objections. Just remember to breathe, repeat the objection (if stated verbally) and ask Who, What, When, Where, How & Why questions to uncover the real objection.

Then ask "If I could...would you?" (If I could help you lower your cost and increase your savings, would you allow me too?)

Get a strong commitment.

Shake their hand.

Tell them you appreciate them.

This Sales Process works if you work it!

If in your first 30 days, you have difficulty with the process or need some clarification from (9am to 9pm est.), call, (770) 873-1931 and I will help you review THE BOOK.
*Please <u>read</u> the Book completely first.
*Please do not call while with your customer. This would be unprofessional and make you look like an amateur. If you can't reach me leave a message and I will return it when I'm free, usually in the same day.

You are welcome to email me at <u>derekstaden@yahoo.com</u> with questions.

I believe in you, I hope you believe in you. Let's get you across that finish line!

- Derek

Notes:

-

-

-

- <u>Useful Scripts</u>

1) Script for Door to Door sales

(Knock) "Hello, Sir/Ma'am my name is (Your Name). I am with (Name of Organization) and we are completing a short survey in the community this week to improve the quality of life of the residence of our neighborhood and would like to see if you could help us out?"

(Shut up and W.F.A. "Wait for Answer")

If the answer is "Yes" then proceeding by sharing quickly who the Company is, the Concepts and the Support that you are looking for from the Neighbor.

If the answer is "No" then proceed by: leaving a sample of product (If applies), a business card, and get permission to revisit them at a better time for the prospect.

Your neighborhood Survey should be no more than 5 questions beginning with one of these words

"Who, What, When, Where, How or Why?"

2) Script for Phones

"Hello this is _____, I met you a couple of days ago at (Remind them where), do you remember me? (WFA) Great! I was just following up with you as I promised, by the way do you have a quick second to talk?

Fantastic! Well…I will not keep you long. I promised I would follow up with you…and I only have a couple of quick questions and I will get out of your way, is that ok?

First, I work with some very successful people that I network with from time to time. They always ask me to keep my eyes open for specific types of people.

There are (3) top attributes that we look for in people so when I say what they are please let me know of the first person that comes to mind, sound fair? WFA. Great!

I can't make any promises, if they are a fit, I will pass their name on. Sound fair? WFA.

Ok. So… the first person that we look for is a great teacher. So, when I say the word "Teacher" who is the first person that comes to mind? WFA. Thank you.

Ok. The second type of individual that we look for is a highly enthusiastic person. So, when I ask, who is the most Enthusiastic person that you know…who comes to mind?

WFA. Great Thank You.

One last question, who is the most Ambitious person that you know?

Thank you, by the way for taking my call. I can't make any promises that the names that you provided would be interested **or** if we would be interested **in them** but we would like to share some information with you and have you pass it along to them, about our Company and see if you could get permission for us to call them. Our goal is to see if they would be interested or if they could point us in the right direction to someone that may be, does this sound fair?

(They respond: *What is this? What do you do?) You reply: **Why** are you asking for <u>you</u> or <u>someone else</u>? WFA Great! as I shared early I can't promise you (or your friend) anything, because we are looking for a specific type of person.

So, we would like to meet them and provide some information and ask some important questions before we commit to anything. But, I would like to meet with you in the next day or two to put some information in your hands. You are welcome to pass it along to your friends or family that you think may be a fit. Our goal is to get permission to contact them and see if they have questions or any interest. Sound Fair? WFA,

Ok, I will be back in the area that where I met you, in the next couple of days…I would like to meet you somewhere near there for a cup of coffee and I can provide information about what we are looking for and we can address any questions that you have, I have some time on Monday if that's okay or is Wednesday better? WFA. Great!

Ok, are the mornings okay or would the afternoon be better? WFA. Fantastic!

So, around 1pm okay or would 3 pm be better? Great!

Now please make a quick note of the date and time of our meeting, I will hold while you grab a pen and a piece of paper okay?

Ok…the place is _____ the date is _____ the time is _____ my name is spelled (spell your name) and you have my number?

(If you want to be certain they have your info, ask them to **repeat the information**)

I look forward to seeing you again. I really enjoy meeting new people and working in the community. I know you are a person of your word, as I am a person of my word…so if anything were to come up please call me as far in advance as possible to let me know and we can reschedule. I will do the same. Unless there is a life or death issue that comes up, I will be there on time.

I thank you for your time. I hope you enjoy the rest of your day/night? See you on…"

Second Script:

"Hello this is _____ with ABC Company in Atlanta, is (John or Mary) there?

Key: Make a statement then, ask a question. (See above)

Great! The reason for my call is your name was passed on to me as someone that may be interested in the widget, that our company creates, is that correct?

Fantastic! If you are like me you don't make a decision without a lot of information, is that correct? Yes! So, we will be in your area on Tuesday demonstrating the widget, to other interested consumers and would like to know if Tuesday would be ok to pop by to see you or would Thursday be better?

Key: Give a choice for date/time for the appointment. It's a "Pop by" (quick stop), never a meeting (long visit)!

Wonderful! We will see you Tuesday at 6pm. Please we can only visit with you if all decision makers are there to ensure that we address all questions and concerns. So, I will hold while you grab a pen and piece of paper to jot down my name and contact information.

Script: Ok great, my name is __, my number is __, our appointment date is __.

I have a few stops on Tuesday, so please call as far in advance as you can in the event that we need to reschedule. I usually keep my phone on vibrate when I stop to visit with a potential client so, I may not get your call or message if you call during the day of our visit. Also, I will not call you the day of our appointment unless I need to reschedule. I will be here at the agreed upon time, is that ok?" Sounds Great! Thank them & hang up.

Discussion: This script is obviously for a certain type of client. More of a direct sale. But it can be tweaked to work with an insurance appointment, a real estate appointment, carpet cleaning service, frozen foods truck, water filters, gutter cleaner...the options are endless.

I am only mentioning a handful of careers but there are so many that you could make a great living as a sales professional in. Just keep your eyes open and breathe!

3) Script for Referrals

"Ma'am/Sir now that you have decided to move forward with our service, I would like to say, thank you for your trust and if I could, may I please have your Driver's License(s) so, I may complete your agreement? Thank You.

By the way, (while looking at the identification provided) ask...is this your correct mailing address? phone number?

"Thanks. John/Mary, I can only stay in business by providing an extreme value to my clients and getting referrals. I usually ask from those who see value for themselves and that would like to share this information with their loved ones and friends to provide at least 10 or more referrals during your appointment. Most times my clients will search their cell phone directory, could you please jot down at least 10 names and numbers to help me with my business, keeping in mind, that we will treat them with the same respect that we provided to your family?"

4) Script for Close

"Now that we've had the opportunity to find out more about you and your family, I would like to share a little bit about myself and the company that I represent. Would that be ok?

Great! (Share 5 minutes or less on the Company, Concepts & Customer Service. Also, tell how you got involved and your plans with the organization)

"Now that you know a little bit about us, let me share our wonderful service/product with you.

We covered how our product works, as well as the features and benefits to you and your family. I would like to ask you if our product can provide those benefits that would fill your current needs and not have any of the drawbacks of your current product, what would prevent you from allowing us to help you today?"

Notes:

-

-

-

-

-

-

-

Who is a Salesperson?

Who is a salesperson? The better question is..."Who is **not** a Salesperson?" All of us buy and sell our opinions, products and information every day!

We search endlessly through our phone, tablet, or laptop seeking information or searching for things to solve our daily issues online. Once we find it...we take it as gospel! Is that a fair statement?

It has been said in the industry that salespeople are the easiest people to sell "anything" too. We don't double verify the information or go to the library to research the data. We just simply accept it as fact.

We gobble up the information, and that's that. What if, learning how to becoming a Superstar in direct or consultative sales was that easy? Well...it can be!

When we realize that people want their problems solved (with information or products) and they are willing to pay someone to solve them, the question is…

"Will you be there when it's time to fill that potential customers need?

I believe that you CAN properly prepare so you can seize the opportunity when it is CREATED.

I said CREATED because, you will have to DO certain things to cause these opportunities to exist. One of those things is to become a professional in your field. So, what do I mean by that?

Here's what I mean:

Know your product/service as well as anyone else. Be prepared to handle objections to your customer **not** wanting to buy your product or service.

Be good at asking questions and taking note of the response.

Be mindful of what is important to your potential client. Listen and they will tell you.

Ask for the sale, with the confidence that you will get the sale.

Get referrals from each prospect whether a sale is made or not!

Men as Salespeople

Sleek-suited, fit man, complete with dress hat and nice dress shoes. This is just one of the glamorous images of the ancient salesman. He smokes, drinks and indulges in other worldly vices. He is highly confident, fairly intelligent (so he thinks so) and quick witted. Admired by men & desired by women. Nowadays, salesmen work in cubicles, work from home, travel from business to business or door to door selling their wares. No more suits. They wear khaki pants and pullover shirts.

Gone are the days when you needed a closet full of high-end suits to exude power to impress your potential clients.

If you are getting sales results these days, your clothes, shoes and even your hairstyles are negotiable. Just dress neat, be well groomed, know your customer & your product and have a warm smile.

Women as Salespeople

What a turnaround! Women once played second fiddle to men in the sales marketplace. Not anymore! Now, women are some of its greatest leaders.

Due to a women's often times keenly developed skill of multi-tasking; as it relates to managing a household, women are excelling as Sales Professionals over men.

Women tend to dress the part more consistently, have a higher percentage that are educated within their profession and due to sales being mostly commission based, equal pay is not much of an issue.

Ladies, you can learn this business and master it. Believe in yourselves, know your products and set aggressive goals that allow you to win your life back and give you more time freedom.

Young People in Sales

Are you kidding me? What could be any more of a slam-dunk than a cute kid offering you to buy from his/her catalog so that can go on a school field trip or cookies to raise money for their organization.

Young people are extremely confident and have not lived long enough to be negatively affected in the same way as adults by the word "No".

So, with the proper supervision your child could get a lemonade stand, cookie or lawn care business and become successful at sales very early in life, which could lead to great opportunities in the future.

Millennial Salespeople

Okay. This one is tricky. I have worked with several Millennials in the past 5 years. What I've learned is quite a bit. I started out attempting to conform them to my way of doing business and was met with refusal at every turn.

Eventually I discovered that the best way to influence this group is to find a "Willing" millennial participant and teach them everything you know. Ensure that you gently deal with correcting them as they tend to shut down quickly when it appears that you are forcing them to conform to any measurable structure. Accountability, Discipline and Structure is "Greek" to most.

Having measurable goals allows the goals to do all the correcting as oppose to the coach "lashing out" when the salesperson doesn't work as diligently as the leader desires.

It goes without saying that with social media at their disposal Millennials could become formidable global sales professionals.

Sell for Cash vs. Selling to Solve Problems

When I first got involved in professional sales it was all about the money! How much could I make and how fast could I make.

As I observed other salespeople making mistakes and recognized that I was unconsciously selling for cash, I decided to make a change.

I started looking for mentors to help teach me how to speak, dress and service my clients like a "true" professional.

After several books, cassettes, C.d.'s and DVD's, I finally found a strong teacher. He taught me how to study my craft and my clients so I could develop satisfied customers that are willing to provide REFERRALS. This coaches' guidance changed my business and my life.

I figured out in short order that solving my client's issues were my focus and getting referrals, my ultimate goal.

Learning the Sales Process

I have had several sales trainees, mention how difficult it is for them to learn the sales process. Some say it's harder than learning how to stop smoking cigarettes.

Remember, the difficulty with learning a new process is usually due to the system in which you are attempting to learn it thru, being jacked up!

You can have success with this system. Just trust the information. I did and it worked (And is working) for me and others.

Trusting the process

There is a process to getting referrals and reaching a sell. If you don't believe this then, you must believe that it, (your success) is purely a matter of chance.

This is not the way to mentally approach such a highly rewarding career. There are manuals or guides to most professions. Doctors have them, Ministers have them (Bible) and Lawyers have them.

People that have come before us, wrote down their experiences so that we could have a track to run on. Remember, that there is nothing new under the sun.

There is not an easy way to reach your goals but there is a simpler way. Don't change your product or services. No one knows what product will be hot or when it will fall out of favor with the public. Its about you.

So, when you are installing this sales system, stick to it at least 90 days first before you change to a "new system" or switch which products you offer.

90 days gives you a chance to tweak the system to fit your personality.

<u>Save 20% of your earnings</u>

This one is straight-forward and should be non-optional. Sales can be up and down (a little bit) when you are first installing your sales system. It is great to have a few thousand dollars to fall back on, in a pinch. Life will happen, please be prepared.

Save Money & Buy Stuff

Now, this will sound a little contradictory. Saving money is very important. But for some sales people, spending 10-15% each paycheck is just as important. You see, once you spend a few dollars, you have to replace them! So, save money but ALSO go...buy some STUFF!

Willingness

Without this one trait, it will be impossible to accomplish the goals that you set for you Sales business. Most people want to, but they lack the willingness to see it thru.

Do "IT" Daily

Whatever activities lead you closer to your Goals and Dreams, never neglect to do some or all of them daily. This may sound insensitive...as you say "Derek I have a LIFE"! I understand but, having a "special life" requires an "exchange" of one thing for another. Some call it sacrifice.

Important Terms

Hot Potato

This is the name we give to "deflecting a question". Why call it "Hot Potato"? The reason is this, whenever a prospective client asks you a question that you need time to answer, you would throw back a question.

Remember whoever is asking questions is in control. Sure, Mom said never answer a question with a question. But in this case, it will be alright.

Remember: **Questions** not Statements **control a sales conversation**. Never forget this. "If you speak you only hear what you already know but if the client speaks you are learning what's important to them."

Ben Franklin Close

It has been said that Ben Franklin used a certain process when faced with making an important decision.

He would take a piece of paper, draw two lines on it in the form of a giant capital letter "T". On the left side of the paper would be the "Pro's" and on the right, would be the "Con's". He would ask himself what are the advantages and disadvantages to agreeing to a particular decision.

This is a great way to illustrate to your clients why they should buy your product or service. You illustrate all the "Pro's" or reasons why they **should** buy from you then, you put down the pen and ask them to come up with all the "Con's", or why they **shouldn't** buy from you.

Whichever list is longer should be the way that they should go! If you have a great product then you shouldn't worry.

"Yes" Momentum

When you are properly using the art of "Asking Questions", you will lead your prospective clients to a "Yes" decision more effectively through the Sales Process.

The way that this is done is after the presentation is given, you would ask questions that could only have a "yes" or "no" answer.

The key to this is to ask obvious "Yes" answer questions.

IE: (For example)

Do you care about the financial, spiritual and emotional well-being of your family?

Do you want what's best for them?

You reviewed the benefits of our product; did you see any value for you & your family?

If I could help you get a product that provides more value and cost less than your current product is there any logical reason why I couldn't earn your business today? W.F.A. Great!

I also understand that If you are like me you probably don't make a decision without a lot of information. So, I would like to provide that information for you. After we do that if feel that it makes sense, adds value and saves you money do you see any logical reason why we can provide you more information?

WFA. Fantastic!

Alternative Choice Close

This is one of my favorite closing techniques. It requires extreme faith in your product or service. If you have that then this will probably be your number #1 closing technique. I use it primarily to make appointments.

Here's how:

"Sir what is best for you is Monday ok? or would Wednesday be better to sit down with you and your spouse to discuss the plan I have to show you?"

The choices are endless. This can be used for closing at any point in the process. The genius in this is that it is simple. The option that you are offering is "Yes" or "Yes"!

If I could...would you?

Sales to an extent is manipulation for the benefit of the person that you are trying to help with your product or service. This closing technique is very affective.

Here's an example:

"If I could provide all of the features and value that you said you are missing in your current product and at the same time provide none of the things that you dislike about your current product, would you let me help your family today?"

Open-probe questions

These are questions that are to be used during the opening phase of the presentation. They are purely utilized to uncover the needs and wants of the client.

Open-probe questions are:

Who? What? When? Where? How? & Why?

For example:

Who is on that picture over the mantle?

What do you like best about your current product?

When did you purchase it?

Where are your insurance policies, I want to provide you with a complimentary analysis of your coverage?

How did you meet your last Real Estate agent?

Close-probe questions

When you move to the closing phase, things can change somewhat.

Now we will use open-probe questions to ask closing questions.

Examples are:

How would you like to pay?

Who would like to complete the application?

What would be a good time to have our personnel office to call to confirm your banking info?

F.O.R.M.

Family /Occupation /Recreation /Motivation

An acronym used to remember the best way to open up a conversation with a prospective client.

Example:

Is your **family** from this area?

Where do you **work**?

What do you do when you're **not** working?

What is your **greatest** motivation?

(Not only will these questions produce excellent answers that can help you understand your clients needs better, but also help you make a sell & get referrals)

If you discover that they have several family members in the area, they work at a huge company where they are very well liked and when they aren't working they go to large gatherings on a regular basis...It could be extremely beneficial! Dig...Probe...Find the Treasure! That's why its called prospecting.

S.T.E.A.M.

This is a great way to pick up referrals.

When you get past your first phase, of becoming a sales professional, you will need to find someone to train...(and a process to gain more clients). Let your WARM contacts know that your business depends on obtaining referrals & trainee's daily.

"I usually only ask for 30 referrals upfront. After I prove my value…my clients offer me more, and I offer nice incentives. So, who do you know that would like to save money or make more money?"

The growth of your business and thereby your income relies on finding good quality people to teach your system too.

So…How do you find them? Look to your greatest asset, your clients!

Who do you know that is a….

Salesperson
Teacher
Enthusiastic
Ambitious &…
Money-Motivated

(Be very descriptive: "Motivated Salesperson?", "Effective Teacher?", "Who is the most Enthusiastic person you know?" etc…)

*Feel free to add your style to these scripts. Be natural with it. Have fun.

As you go through your presentations with your prospective clients, they will learn about your Company, Concepts and How you get paid.

People like to Make, Save & Protect their Money so if they ask…let them know "that it is YOUR Goal to help THEIR family?"

Notes:

We really enjoyed writing this guide. We love to hear your stories of success and even your challenges. If you have a special client upcoming call us. We would love to mental encourage you and possible give some pointers (or remind you of what paragraphs to refresh on).

Everything you need is in here!

If you need help (first 90 days) I will make myself available for you. Keep Pushing! 770-873-1931 (10am-5pm Est) or by email: derekstaden@yahoo.com

In Business

2 Slow is Painful

The Deluxe Edition

Hello my name is Derek Staden,

I wrote this handy guide to be a quick reference tool, to provide some hope to my friends, partners, and students.

If you are stalled out or treading water in your business this may be exactly what you need.

This guide is designed to get you moving toward a NEW way of acting while you are developing a new way of THINKING!

We believe that going 2 slow, within a competitive climate, such as the times that we are in today, can be a recipe for disaster.

I am the youngest male of (17) children.

(I was raised with only one of my siblings, my deceased-brother, Christopher Staden)

I am originally from Jackson, Ga and I was raised in Decatur, Ga. (near Atlanta).

Our family struggled financial but we were all dedicated entrepreneurs and hard workers.

During high school, I found success in the sport of Wrestling, as well as starting in (2) other varsity sports (Baseball & Football).

I am a medically-Retired (Wartime) Veteran, of the U.S. Air Force.

My (primary) careers have been in the Military, Money Management, Music & Marketing.

(I have an extensive background in negotiations, promotions, sales, sales coaching, sales training, and advertising as well)

I am a full-time teacher, mentor, & loyal friend.

I was fortunate to attended (5) post-high school graduate programs. I have only completed (3) of them. (My Biblical/Torah Hebrew Studies, PFS University (obtained my 6 & 63, Life & Health, P & C, & Mortgage Brokers Licensing), as well as the completion of an Aeronautical Sciences program provided to me while in the Air Force, (from a local Community College).

All of this education and training took a while to accomplish. Most people complete their post-high school education in 4-8 years. It took me 20 yrs! Lol…(19yrs old to the ripe old age of 39) So never give up!

I was chasing my dreams in the entertainment industry & building a family.

I developed several small business operations. Some did okay and unfortunately some did poorly.

Even through all of this, my former spouse was able to open her own commercial & residential cleaning business.

We also, encouraged several friends to develop small businesses during some very rough times.

Now that I have a chance to reflect back on it I am shocked at our results, considering we spent a lot of our time doing activities that were counter-productive to reaching our long-term goals.

Although, this seems like a full and rewarding life, times were very challenging for us. We had to fight through fear every day. We had to develop mental strength to combat stress and anxiety. There were times that I wanted to quit and go back to a J.O.B. (almost every day).

Sounds like I should be content and relaxed now that I am retired. I am not! Although I am on track to receive a couple of million dollars, over the next 40 years, I am far from comfortable.

All I need to do is I simply wake up, maintain my health and live a low-stress existence for the next 40 plus years (or so) and enjoy my family: (Mom, Kids and Grandkids) and friends.

SO WHATS MY PROBLEM?

I don't think I can stop caring about other people's problems. I love helping people. I enjoy seeing people's eyes light up when they talk about their dreams and goals.

It bothers me when people suffer.

I must be cursed. I should be out taking a walk, or on a deep-sea fishing trip. I should be traveling extensively. Sleeping more. I also, could stand to lose a few extra pounds.

So, why can't I just disconnect and relax? Why can't I just accept my current financial situation?

What makes me stay up late thinking about other people's dreams & goals? Why do I care when my students (at the Paradigm Brothers Development School, in Harvey Louisiana), ask for EXTRA help? Why do I feel the need to get involved…for FREE after they have completed their training?

Most people in my circle are seeking financial (time) freedom, what…am I seeking???

My original Purpose for this Guide:

My original thought was this book will inspire my friends and partners who are currently feeling overwhelmed or stressed. This is for my friends that I am aggravating (that are also frustrating me). I sometimes feel that I want them to WIN more than they want too. This can't be true of course, although it surely seems that way at times.

What is it then?

They are ACTING like anchors grounding our ship called, "Financial Independence". I would rather them act like the wind, to the sails of OUR tremendous ship.

They seem to understand that we need to be profitable. They even know HOW to make money. They all have done it in the past or they are making decent incomes now.

So, why don't I allow them to go at their own slow pace? I know that it can be counter-productive to "push people" when they are acting reluctant.

Unless you are "Pushing People Up"!!!

So, what am I thinking?

Do WE lack the knowledge on how to properly leverage other people's time & resources? Do we focus on the path of least resistance which is to focus on Direct Sales or our J.O.B. security?

We talk to the same people, expecting them to wake up and allow us to "help" them with our businesses by buying some more PRODUCTS???

I say talk to everyone, get a NO or fight to get a YES, then you can move on. This way you will have little to no Regret.

You could avoid building a relationship with your clients? How about we do nothing, that way we can AVOID objections & rejection completely???

We should focus on adding extreme VALUE! Most people do a poor job of providing more value than they promise. We want a full reward without paying a full price. Are we thieves?

We must care about our client's well-being as much as our own. We must aggressively show this in our ACTIONS not just in our words or with our presentations.

WE must spend quality time with our clients and demonstrate better follow up.

We must also, talk to NEW people every day. WE need our businesses to grow. It takes developing new relationships while building on the current relationships.

We must also get more referrals from everyone, (As long as they see a benefit in our offerings).

We should call the referrals before the satisfied client that provided them to you, becomes disappointed with your follow through skills.

We need to SAVE, INVEST & PROTECT the money we earn, for our futures as well as our family's futures.

Why are we talking, thinking and ACTING so, slowly?

Maybe we are happy with our moderate results and we feel as though we have arrived, so **now** we can relax? Woah!

You should Love what you do **OR** you should stop doing it.

Go BIG or GO home!!!

So why do we need to go FASTER?...

1) Why go FASTER?

2) What should we be doing FASTER?

3) When should we "Slow Down" then?

4) How to track if we're moving FAST(ER)?

5) Who should we go FASTER with?

"Its not how much money we make, but it's more about how we make it and what we do with it"

So, on the next few pages we will give an outline to this plan to "go faster" which should allow you to avoid so much pain.

Hopefully we can focus on seeking pleasure while building your amazing business.

Why should you go faster?

There is a period of time in the beginning that a business much do quite a bit, to establish its proper foundation, develop its systems and prepare to grow relationships that cater to your client's needs.

1) Set Up and Plan for the "End Game".
(Business & Action Planning)

2) Gather resources and Manpower.

3) Delegate the "work" needed by the organization.

4) Set goals to and actively pursue prospective clients.

5) Get massive referrals and testimonials.

6) Make money (the plan is to make a nice profit)

7) Pay your corporate taxes, expenses

8) Put away for short & long-term savings needs.

9) Review results. Make adjustments.

10) Determine if you are on track to reaching your stated goals.

*If your business is not on track, you may be thinking, acting and speaking to slow. Remember your competitors are watching.

Here is the Issue:

We set Goals that we usually don't completely achieve anyway. So, even if we set appropriate goals... called S.M.A.R.T. goals that are:

Specific

Measurable

Attainable

Realistic

Time-Bound

Yet, we still seem to be behind our stated goals for the year???

So, if you are not meeting your objectives for financial, spiritual or physical needs...it may be time to change the TEMPO of your ACTIVITY!

Because 2 slow can be Painful!!!

Slow-thinkers give off a raw offensive stench to the nostrils of high-achievers. Slow-thinkers and Slow-talkers meander along in complete and total mediocrity. "We will get a round to it", "Just take your time", "We are doing okay", "WE will be just fine…I promise".

Slow-thinkers sometimes confuse "Moving FASTER" with doing MORE work. This is the flaw of the inexperienced. This could be further from the truth. The only person that will work HARDER is a driven, excited and positive person. (Sometimes a fearful, stressed out and externally-motivated person will also)

So, do only what you love!

Our goal isn't to work MORE but, in a more stream-lined way.

A.   We should pay people outside of the organization to complete task that are simple management tasks. ($10/hr. is fair)

B. We should shift our focus to using our advanced skills to CREATE new relationships and revenue! (Not to manage)

C. Workers have J.O.B.s but Bosses create!

Are you a BOSS or not?

If, during the stream-lining of your process, you begin to identify, that your results (which are attached to your clients & partners goals) appear destined to fall short, you may realize that you are setting yourself up for FAILURE.

Of course, you don't desire this reality. So, if you find yourself working with SLOW-THINKERS, what could you do?

You could run away immediately! Cancel the business deal? Create new alliances! Force everyone away (run them off). Or Quit???...OR

You could try to infect them with your thinking…this sometimes works.

You could affect them with your ACTIONS…this rarely works.
Lastly, you could ask for a change to the partnership or a raise??? (Interesting)

Let's talk about Multiple-Streams of Income

-Most people have Direct or Linear Income.

-Even less have Residual Income.

-Even fewer have Leveraged or Passive income.

-And rarely do we receive Windfall income.

Here are the income percentages from a friend, from the past 12 months:

0% of his income form Direct Sources

20% from Leveraged or Passive Sources

70% from Residual sources and

10% from Windfall sources

He <u>still</u> isn't happy with this!
His next (12) month Goals are:

10% from Direct Sources

50% from Leveraged or Passive Sources

40% from Residual Sources and

10% from Windfall Sources

Wow, this makes too much sense.

If you fail in Business, your Passive income can come to an END! If you get fired or get sick, your ability to make Direct income can suddenly END! So, we should learn how to leverage other people's skills & abilities then INVEST!

What should WE be doing Faster?

"WE are creators not Managers? So, meet more People

1) Meet (5) people/day, (6) days/wk for (30) days.

2) Set Appointments using only a SCRIPT!

3) Present your (3) C's!
Company/Concepts/Compensation

4) Ask for REFERRALS throughout the presentation.

5) Ask your client for the opportunity to do an Assessment.

6) Set an Appointment to return to provide the best solutions.

7) Return to the client when you have earned the right to ask for business!

8) Get Numbers for the Referrals/then Book them!
9) Follow up with your clients & share the positive results from the Referrals/Thank them.

Now, invite them to visit your office to tour your operations.

When should we "slow-down"?

Slow down once per week (maybe twice if you have a huge operation). You should do this to catch up on your rest, analyze and adjust your activities; to ensure that your T.E.A.M. is on track for the next week, to achieve stated goals.

Here is what you do when you slow down:

1) Meet to inspect your T.E.A.M.'s progress
(Have an Agenda)

2) Ensure all Partners are present.
(Discuss your Results)

3) Analyze your Results & Shortfalls (if any)

4) Create Goals for the next (7) days.
(To secure the Vision)

5) Celebrate the Results.
(Tell everyone on the T.E.A.M.) 6)
Get back to WORK.

7) Communicate DAILY with All Partners
(For Accountability) 8)   Track Results.
(If you are not on track, Go FASTER!)

How do know that we're going FASTER?

"We should keep all of our oars in the water, or we might end up going around in circles"

"Let's use all of the bullets in our weapon, so we can hit more targets and be more productive"

Are we going FASTER?

Let's track our:

Direct Sales _____%

Leveraged or Passive Sales _____%

Residual Income _____%

Windfall Income _____%

(Windfall's could represent the sale of Real Estate, Lottery or Gambling winnings, Life or Annuity proceeds, Gifts & Donations,

Advances on Contracts, Settlements or Lawsuits etc.)

Set a Date to Retire from your J.O.B.

Then tell everyone.

Tell your wife, children, parents, and then post it all over the internet.

Go buy a new(er) car. Buy a house.

Have a baby.

Open a Retirement Account.

Increase your Emergency Savings.

This type of activity will help foster a more positive & exciting atmosphere in your network, which will manifest into a more productive behavior so, you can GO FASTER!

"You are either running from HELL or racing to Heaven in Business"

So, should we go faster?

It depends. Maybe it's a personal choice. I already have passive & residual income. This does not require me to go FASTER (Yet I am more engaged using my FREE time, mentoring students than most teachers I know). Hopefully, this is not by choice.

I don't have a spouse. I don't have dependent children. I have a cheap domestic vehicle. No mortgage. A moderate-sized but cheap apartment. No fancy or expensive clothing. Pretty low expenses other than supporting my friends and family with gifts or attending to an occasional need.

So why not go faster so you can be free(er)???

Now, in defense of my peers, over the next (40) plus years I am scheduled to make over $2 million in residual income.

I also have tons of time available to use on just myself.

I am fortunate to have very high energy for someone my age.

I have been told I possess strong business skills.

I tend to come out on the positive side, when I negotiate deals.
I have been told I am a decent Sales Professional.

I coach and teach Sales & Business Development almost daily.

My goal is to be supportive, I am often tough when I train or coach (but fair) & I am a loving friend.

I get turned on by helping others. I recognize how fortunate I am…but going **2 slow** still feels PAINFUL!!!

Here is why I feel a need to go FASTER:

I don't want to depend on a job, the government or anyone for my well-being. I don't want to have my children and grandkids to struggle as my parents and I have, in the past.

What about you, should you go faster?

(Before you answer)

Read this:

"66% of the World Population lives on less than $2 per day."

How do you take care of your basic needs on such a small amount of money?

Don't all humans deserve to have a decent quality of life? What about their dreams? Why do we take our opportunities for granted? We do we feel that the world owes us something? I want you to have a more fruitful life. I want you to have hope that you can achieve your DREAMS.

Believe it or not you are fortunate to live in a time and place that is better than what our parents had. There are so many people that live a horrible existence and survive on love & charity.

Let's end poverty and suffering. Let's go FASTER friends.

-D

Thanks to My Mother (Irma Head Blake) for giving me life, loving me, praying for me, loving and supporting MY children and grandchildren. Being an example for me and my brother. (And for my Mom) teaching my daughter how to be a Lady. Thank you for always supporting my goals and dreams.

Thanks to my Father for giving me life, providing me with wonderful siblings and serving his country diligently.

Thanks to my brother for being with me in my life and after death in my mind and in my heart.

With eternal Love.

-D

(Review this manual at least 3 times, completely, before you call us, this will ensure that you are properly prepared to discuss your questions with us.)

-Thank you
(Derek "Coach Dee" Staden)

GO SEIZE THE DAY!

Written by Derek Staden   Senior Editor: D.Todd Staden

1st Edition created on Jan. 27, 2017   Revised last Dec 31, 2020

Staden's Sales Guide to Riches (2020 Addition)

Original Copywrite © July 2018